ROBERTO'S READABLE RHETORIC

ROBERTO'S READABLE RHETORIC

Robert Nurton

ARTHUR H. STOCKWELL LTD
Torrs Park, Ilfracombe, Devon, EX34 8BA
Established 1898
www.ahstockwell.co.uk

First published in Great Britain, 2019

British Library Cataloguing-in-Publication Data.
A catalogue record for this book is available from the British Library.

FIRST EDITION

Proceeds from the sale of this book
will be donated to the Dogs Trust.

ISBN 978-0-7223-4932-8
Printed in Great Britain by
Arthur H. Stockwell Ltd
Torrs Park Ilfracombe
Devon EX34 8BA

INTRODUCTION

These jokes, epigrams, rhymes and other writings have been collected over a period of years by an ordinary person who hopes they will appeal to ordinary people. There are no gimmicks in this book, no national heroes, no great entertainers – nothing that will really appeal to anybody other than the ordinary person.

So, if you are an ordinary person, and you feel like an ordinary person's laugh, flick through the pages; and if you produce a wry smile or a good belly laugh, it's been worthwhile!

Remember – there's little or nothing new in this world, so just adopt what's there, adapt it and improve it.

Two of the most difficult things to do: climb a wall leaning towards you and kiss a woman leaning away from you.

Wife to husband: "What would you like for breakfast?"

"Soft-boiled egg, please."

A minute later she said, "Come into the kitchen and make mad passionate love to me."

He said, "Why the kitchen?"

She said, "To time the egg!"

A little old man shuffled slowly into an ice-cream parlour and pulled himself slowly and painfully up on to the stool. After catching his breath he ordered a banana split.

The waitress asked kindly, "Crushed nuts?"

"Thank you," he replied, "but it's arthritis!"

A guy goes into a motorway café and asks for a sausage (burnt on the outside and raw inside), a piece of steak so badly burnt you can't eat it, some cold beans and an egg (the white cooked, but not the yolk).

The man behind the counter says, "We can't do that!"

The guy replies, "Why not? You did it yesterday!"

The difference between irritation, aggravation and frustration:

You open a telephone book, pick a number, dial it and say, "Is Alf there?"

"No, no, no," he apologises.

THAT'S IRRITATION.

You dial the same number and say, "Is Alf there?"

He gets upset – "You again!" – and threatens to call the police.

THAT'S AGGRAVATION.

Again you dial the same number and say, "It's Alf here – have there been any calls for me?"

THAT'S FRUSTRATION.

A rabbi is sitting on a train opposite a priest.

"Tell me, Your Worship," the rabbi says, "why do you wear a collar back to front?"

"Because I am a father," answers the priest.

"I am also a father and I don't wear my collar like that."

"Ah," says the priest, "but I am father to thousands."

To which the rabbi replies, "Maybe it's your trousers you should wear back to front!"

Definition of a kipper: two-faced, no guts and permanently pickled.

YOU HAVE HEARD OF PARKINSON'S LAW AND SOD'S LAW, BUT HAVE YOU HEARD OF COLES LAW? NO! IT'S JUST SHREDDED CABBAGE AND SALAD CREAM.

"I did not go to bed with my wife before we were married – did you?"

"I don't know – what was her maiden name?"

Is a BARBEQUE a line of men waiting for a haircut?

There was an insurance agent who did not know the difference between arson and incest – he went home and set fire to his sister.

A guy was standing in a bar one night talking to a very attractive young lady who was wearing a very, very skimpy tight black dress.

He said to her, "How on earth do you get into that dress?"

She said, "Try two large gin and tonics."

Three Italian women were talking about what famous personality they would like to be. The first woman said she would like to be Sophia Loren because she was very beautiful and had a lot of money. The second woman said she would like to be Jackie Onassis because she travelled the world and also had a lot of money. The third woman said she would like to be Sahara Pipeline and when asked why she said because she was laid by twenty men in six weeks.

The phone rang in the middle of the night.

A man answered and said, "You've got the wrong number – it's the Meteorological Office you want."

His wife said, "Who was that?"

"Chap on the phone wanted to know if the coast was clear."

Superman was talking to Spiderman: "I really fancy Wonder Woman."

Spiderman replied, "Well, look – there on the ground. Go straight down there."

Whoosh, he flew straight down. Whoosh, he came straight back.

"What happened? Did you enjoy yourself?"

"Well, I really gave the Invisible Man a fright."

GOD MADE TIME, BUT MAN MADE HASTE.

I don't know what antibiotics my mother used when I was born, but I am still very confused. I have got so many brains I haven't used half of them yet.

"No! No! A hundred times no," said the centipede, crossing her legs.

What is the similarity between a police constable and a nymphomaniac?

Whenever you want one you can't find one.

I met a chap the other day who thought Harvey's Bristol Cream was a chest liniment for women.

Athletics Anonymous – if you feel like jogging, somebody will come round for a drink and smoke and talk you out of it.

A chap was caught flashing, but was sentenced in the small claims court.

Why do people say you just want to have your cake and eat it too? What use is a cake you can't eat!

The headmistress of a girls' school said to a male friend who was an author, "Would you give a talk to pupils about sex?"

After much persuasion the man agreed. Too embarrassed to tell his wife he told her he was addressing the school on sailing.

After the talk the headmistress met the wife in the street: "Your husband was wonderful yesterday, so illuminating, and I know my girls learnt a lot."

"I can't think how," said the wife. "He has only tried it twice – the first time he was sick and the second time he lost his hat!"

ONLY THE MEDIOCRE ARE AT THEIR BEST.

DOUBLE JEOPARDY

The sky was cloudless. Charles and Liz Panertz approached the castle, parked the car outside and walked into the main hall. The reception there was in full swing and at a glance it was possible to appreciate the magnificent vista across the terrace overlooking the valley which illustrated the panoramic views and the beauty of the area.

The mixture of nationalities was so obvious and the atmosphere was charged with emotion to such an extent that one found oneself enduring the inevitability of speaking to somebody one had never met before who was sometimes in the mixture of three or four languages, the overall tension being broken by the chink of glasses and the amount of champagne which flowed freely.

One waiter, about five feet tall and as broad and of Italian origin, floated in and out, offering the champagne and orange juice to all. He became mortally offended if anyone refused. His demeanour was one of arrogance tempered with stability, giving the impression that he knew his place but wanted to be noticed all the time. Using his size to an advantage, the manoeuvrability achieved was excellent.

After about twenty minutes or so the general babble died down and people started to drift out of the reception and walk towards the main boardroom. The early procession entered the room slowly with a certain amount of dignity.

Liz moved along with the crowd and was seated before the Rabelaisian rush as people jostled for a few remaining seats. Once everyone was seated in the magnificent room, which had a superb ornate ceiling and fantastic chandeliers, a hush fell over the proceedings as a door opened at the far end of the room. The directors appeared and walked towards the main boardroom table, which was at the end of the room raised on a platform. It was a large table with eleven brown leather chairs on each side; an imposing carver chair which looked like a throne was on the end. The slow procession of people, obviously having practised this art of ritual, filed into the room and took their seats, each aware of their precise position.

Charles Panertz, not having attended these meetings before, followed at the rear and took the last vacant seat. He waited while the remainder sat and at that precise moment he had the impression that all eyes were focused on him and waiting. The silence was awe-inspiring, and then the ice was broken by the ferocity of a lot of coughing from the end of the room and eyes were averted for a second. This gave Charles the opportunity he had been waiting for.

"Do I speak?" he whispered to his neighbour.

"Yes," he replied. "Stand up and say how pleased you are to be here, then sit down."

Charles stood up and said how pleased he was to be there and that he looked forward to contributing to the matters in hand. He then sat down. The business then began. Papers for the proposed merger and loans were produced and handed around.

This was all news to Charles and he started to lose interest; his mind was elsewhere. 'If only this meeting could end!' he thought.

His thoughts were interrupted by what only could be interpreted as a command: "Mr Panertz! Your opinion on the extension of the loan to the Algen brothers?"

Thinking, Charles said, "Should we call it in?"

"Yes – good," a voice replied. "Do it, then."

Charles suddenly realised the true implications of his comment; where to start and what to do was a big enough problem, but to put the matter into operation was another because the Algen brothers, Frank and Roy, were friends of his brother and calling in the loan would finish them as far as Charles was concerned. He knew what had to be had to be, but not today at least; he had forty-eight hours to enjoy the plan before it had to be executed.

The loan to the Algen brothers was only a small part of the problem. Charles Panertz was company secretary and director of a company called Contoria Metals, which was a wholly owned subsidiary of Micerca Holdings. Deep down he had heard a rumour that it was proposed to dispose of Contoria Metals.

All matters on the agenda were virtually finished when Ann Suizet, managing director of Micerca Holdings, said, "The decision has been made to dispose of Contoria Metals Limited. A satisfactory deal has been agreed. All personnel involved in the company will hear officially during the course of the next few days. I therefore now declare this meeting closed."

As you can imagine, this was a complete shock to Charles, who stood there for a moment or two completely bewildered.

Recovering, he walked over to Ann Suizet and asked her, "What on earth is going to happen to me?"

She looked him in the eye coldly and said, "Regretfully, Charles, you will be going. I won't say you will be getting a golden handshake, but you may certainly be getting a silver one."

She then walked out of the room.

Contoria Metals was Charles's life. He had been involved in the company for some twenty years and had worked very hard with Ann Suizet's father, Alfred. When he died Ann inherited the company, and the last two or three years had been very painful for Charles, but he had lived in hope that as he was getting near retirement things would only get better. In fact they got worse.

He clearly did not know what to do, but decided that he would reflect, consider his situation and take advice.

Close friends advised him to take a holiday, have a couple of weeks abroad and come back to reconsider the situation. This seemed good advice, so Charles decided to proceed along these lines.

In the office the following day he heard a whisper that Ann Suizet was going abroad on holiday and he thought he heard the word Majorca mentioned.

An idea whizzed through his mind. 'No,' he thought, 'it is crazy to think along those lines. However, the opportunity may arise. . . .'

When he arrived home that evening he confirmed that within two or three months he would be out of a job. He suggested to his wife about having a holiday for a few days to get away somewhere, and she agreed.

At short notice it was very difficult for him to get reservations, but he was advised of a bucket travel shop, so he went along, approached through the shop door past a row of men and women who appeared to be dealing with tickets and passports, up the staircase through a push-button entrance and up another three flights of winding stairs into a room full of characters of all shapes and sizes. It appeared almost a revolting atmosphere, reeking of garlic and stale sweat. Someone indicated for him to go to the head man's office, which was a converted shop parlour with a semicircular desk. The walls were patterned in terrible paper. There was an incredible portrait hanging behind the manager. The beady eyes of the portrait seemed to follow Charles around the room. After considerable negotiation, he managed to obtain two tickets to Palma to be collected at the airport for a reasonable fee, staying in what appeared to be a good hotel.

Charles and Liz Panertz arrived at the airport and the atmosphere was humid. There was a complete cacophony of sound – what with the airport announcements, multilingual conversations and people of all nationalities hurrying to various destinations. Charles felt completely overwhelmed. He was somewhat concerned when he noticed the passengers queuing for tickets and jostling for position in his particular queue. He thought he might reach the desk only to find out the seats had already been allocated. He hoped desperately that his seats had not been double-booked.

While waiting, he looked around the airport, taking in people and their various attitudes. An oriental couple were passing through, weighed down with luggage but still managing to walk along eating ice cream. A young man bounded up the steps three at a time, his eye on an attractive brunette wearing a backless dress and fishnet stockings. The dress seemed to accentuate her left arm, which was encased in plaster from her fingers to her elbow. Why was he running? Was he chasing her? Or was it the coloured girl in the bright-yellow catsuit pushing a suitcase on wheels at the top of the stairs? Charles's mind buzzed and buzzed and suddenly a posse of Japanese tourists scurried across the walkway, disturbing all before them.

Charles eventually arrived at the counter to collect his tickets and they were there. He and Liz boarded the aircraft and had very comfortable seats, much to Charles's surprise.

'Time to relax,' he thought.

Following the take-off Charles decided he would have a rest. He shut his eyes and went to sleep, and when he woke the scenery from the aircraft was breathtaking. They appeared to be over snow-covered mountains, the sun highlighting the peaks and also picking out what appeared to be skiers. The interruption of the silence was the crew announcing in various languages the dos and don'ts of oxygen masks and escape hatches. Then the sheer beauty of crossing the Alps in full magnificence was indescribable. The patterns looked like a spider's web intricately produced, and the dispersed homes seemed like trapped flies. The whole scene fell away to lush green hills at the side of a lake and to forests edging the complete picture.

As the plane climbed to a higher altitude Charles was left only with the white cloud base, which was broken by a blue effect giving the impression that they were now over the ocean. Unfortunately this was not the case. The reality was that they were flying over clouds and gradually nosing their way through, giving the impression that the plane was surrounded by effervescent soapsuds. The clouds breaking across the windows left him with a feeling of apprehension, unaware of what they would see once they had descended. The anticipation became almost unbearable.

Charles was deep in thought. A cold wind appeared to have blown up, which was blowing the clouds away. With the breaks in the clouds one could see the land and civilisation once again. Charles felt more relaxed.

He turned to Liz and said, "I think we will enjoy ourselves."

Upon landing, the transfer from the airport to the hotel was very quick and efficient, and when Charles and Liz arrived at the hotel the receptionist asked Charles to fill in the usual form, giving his home address and passport number, which he did. As he was doing this he happened to glance at the desk and noticed there was another form which had recently been filled in, and to his amazement and macabre pleasure he noticed the name Suizet.

They were then shown to their room, which basically was pretty adequate, basked in plastic refinements with a very small wardrobe.

Leaving their cases, they went down to what was termed The Clock Bar. It was now 6.30 in the evening. There was a piano being strummed in the background. The bar was completely covered in various clocks of all shapes, sizes, ages and, one could say, different countries, telling the time in virtually every country in the world. The bar seemed so much more elegant than their room – there were sumptuous leather chairs, chesterfields. A young barman was surreptitiously blowing smoke away from the bar counter. It was almost reminiscent of

England in the twenties and Charles half expected the pianist to play 'As Time Goes By'! Strangely enough, the people at the bar seemed to blend in with that period.

Charles and Liz ordered a drink and Charles reflected on what could possibly be in the future. His mind was working overtime. Here was an opportunity; he was in a hotel with his wife, nobody knew where they were, and yet the woman who made his life a complete misery was staying in the same hotel. Could he exact revenge for what she had done to him?

As he sipped his drink, a plan began to evolve. He decided to keep it to himself and not mention a word to Liz.

Amongst the attractions in the hotel was a health-and-leisure complex, which was very fashionable. Charles decided to investigate. It was approached through a long corridor with glass on each side, which gave the impression of a luxurious greenhouse effect. The furniture on the way was Tudor antique and very attractive. In the actual health club the swimming pool itself was kidney-shaped and very large and full of people, mainly very noisy ladies who were swimming almost in convoy up and down and down and up, not allowing anybody else to concentrate on their swimming. Charles decided to try swimming across the pool and was greeted with a language he did not understand, but he knew it left a lot to be desired. It transpired that these ladies and gentlemen came every morning to the pool and if anybody interrupted their swimming between 8.30 and 9.30 a.m. life was not worth living.

Charles got out of the pool and went into the sauna. He was sitting there comfortably when the door was swung open by what can only be described as a charming old lady with a slight hunchback. She turned out to be English. Her vicious northern tongue took command; if there had been no room to sit anywhere else, Charles got the impression that she would have sat on his lap before he had a chance to move. The atmosphere in the sauna appeared to be one of antagonism, and if anyone dared to say anything they were not exactly ignored – they were just sat on. Charles, however, realised this was a situation where he could possibly get his revenge on Ann Suizet. The sauna looked a good place and he knew that Ann Suizet had used the health club; all he had to do was find out the time when she would be there. He hoped she would be on her own, and he was fully aware that the best time would be late in the evening. How to do it? That was the question.

He watched the health club with a certain amount of apprehension and decided it would be sometime that week – as early as possible. He noticed that Ann Suizet was in the health club almost every evening around 5 p.m.; she had a swim and then spent half an hour in the sauna, and it appeared that at this time of the day the swimming pool and sauna were otherwise completely deserted, so Charles decided to act.

Seeing her in the pool, he slipped off his tracksuit, slipped into the water unobserved, swam towards Ann and pulled her under, holding her down until she stopped breathing. Looking around and seeing the pool was still empty, he carried her to the sauna, laid her carefully on the bench, covered her with a towel, turned up the heat and left quietly. Drying himself off quickly, he dressed and went into the gym. He stepped on to the running machine and worked up a considerable sweat. After some thirty minutes he had a quick shower and returned to his room, where Liz was having a snooze and did not even notice he had been away for some while.

When they went down to dinner that evening they were informed of the tragedy and that the local police were asking questions as to what everybody was doing around 5–5.30 p.m. They appeared to be unable to obtain any witnesses whatsoever. Apparently they concluded that Ann Suizet had been swimming, had taken in a lot of water, lay in the sauna and subsequently died. The question of a post-mortem did not even arise. Charles appeared very upset and it was Liz who calmed him down.

"We must enjoy the remainder of our holiday," she said – which they did.

They returned home and naturally felt they had to attend Ann Suizet's funeral when it was announced, which they did.

But to their amazement Ann Suizet appeared and greeted them with the words "I'm so pleased to see you here. You obviously heard of the tragic death of my twin sister. Enjoy your retirement."

A cricketer's wife is in hospital expecting a baby. He goes down to the pub and orders a couple of gin and tonics and then rings the hospital.

"Is there any news?" he asks.

The midwife says, "Yes, you have twins, but there is more to come."

He goes back to the pub and has a few more gin and tonics and rings again, saying to the midwife, "Any news?"

"Ah, yes, you are now the father of quads, but there is still more to come."

Now he gets really drunk and goes to ring the hospital, but accidentally rings the cricket club and says, "What's the score now?"

A voice shouts down the phone, "They're all out and the last one's a duck."

The vicar was playing tennis at a local tennis club and he was not very good at all. He kept getting beaten, but everybody tolerated this and accepted it apart from one objectionable youth.

When the youth came off the court after beating the vicar 6–0, 6–0, he said to him, "What, no miracles today, then, vicar?"

The vicar replied, "I cannot perform miracles, but if you get your mother and father to call and see me I will marry them!"

A chap playing tennis was told by his mother to get home quickly after the game as he had to go to a cocktail party. He rushed off the court and realised that he still had the tennis balls. He put them straight into his pocket and went straight to the cocktail party.

An attractive young lady spoke to him and said, "What is that?"

He replied, "My tennis balls."

"Oh," she said, "is it worse than tennis elbow?"

What do you do when your opponent in golf claims to have found his ball, which was in the rough, and you know he is lying because his ball is in your pocket?

A man was shipwrecked on a desert island for two years and all of a sudden a blonde in a wetsuit came walking on to the island out of the sea. She slowly unzipped her wetsuit and drew out a Mars bar.

"Would you like one?" she said.

The man replied, "Oh yes, please. I haven't seen a Mars bar for two years."

She unzipped a little further and took out a pack of cigarettes.

"Would you like a cigarette?" she said.

"Oh yes, please. I haven't smoked for two years," he replied.

She unzipped even further.

"Would you like to play around?" she said.

"Oh, don't tell me you've got a set of golf clubs in there as well!"

NOTHING COUNTS IN A GAME OF GOLF LIKE YOUR OPPONENT.

There was a young girl from Madras
Who had a most beautiful ass,
But not as you think
(firm, round and pink) –
It was grey, had long ears and ate grass.

There was a monk from Siberia
Whose manners were somewhat inferior.
He did to a nun
What he shouldn't have done
And now she is a Mother Superior.

Twins came and their father, John Dunn,
Gave Edward the name to each son.
When folks said, "Absurd!"
He replied, "Have you heard
That two Eds are better than one?"

A young girl from St Paul
Wore a newspaper dress to ball,
But the dress caught fire
And burnt her entire
Front page, sporting section and all.

A gentle old lady I knew
Was dozing one day in a pew
When the preacher yelled, "Sin!"
She exclaimed, "Count me in
As soon as the service is through!"

IT IS NO EXAGGERATION TO SAY THAT THE UNDECIDED SHOULD GO ONE WAY OR THE OTHER.

LAKELAND BEAUTY

Oh! calm the lake
How green the hills with
mist on high
Low clouds performing ballet
to the tune of the waves
Sun's rays beaming through
the rain, creating the
Sound of silence.

RAIN

Still is the time quiet and lonely
Flowers and shrubs glisten against the light
Vision is impaired but only hazily
Colours change their hue silent and quietly
Knowledge of life appears in the
pools of reflection
Exorcised from the mind is that
which is not clean
Birds and beasts revel, yet dread
the manifestations which ensue
Epitomised in life of everything
in rain.

SNOW

Visions displayed across meadows and woods
are swallowed up in the eternity of loneliness
Engulfed is life – enriched only by
uniformity
Cleverness and simplicity are levelled in
one plane
Vegetation is devoured with
effortless ease
Vigilance against such force is useless
Blanketed is all in the universe
White deserts return rejoicing in
Snow.

FOG

With an aroma of desolation and
confusion
The mist hung low over the
countryside expressing isolation
Visibility was negligible
Bare trees were grotesquely outlined
against the dirty grey pall which
shrouded everything
The music of people and things
is silently stilled
The noises of cattle and birds
normally seen can be heard
eerily muffled by the aura
of density
Now – normally light but clear
discernment is impossible
The obsolescence of the world is seen at
its greatest
When man is reduced to such a
helplessness and stillness by
Fog.

SEASONS

The fields are green in summer
The leaves are on the trees
Roses and other flowers
Rustle in the breeze.

Fields in autumn are bare
Leaves are gone from the trees
Roses and other flowers
Are no longer there.

Fields are white in winter
Trees are shimmering bright
Days are now so short
Much longer is the night.

SEA

The tide came in so gently
It lapped upon the shore
It happened every day like this
One could not ask for more.

The wind sprang up quite mildly
Turning the tide once more
Like a tempestuous child
It lashed the rocks and shore.

The storm blew so roughly
Raging torrents, teeming rain
Turn day into night
Oh for the gentle tide again.

A priest was sent to Alaska. The Bishop visited a year later.

"How do you like it up here?" asked the Bishop.

The priest said, "If it wasn't for my rosary and two Martinis a day I would be lost, Bishop. Would you like a Martini?"

"Yes, thank you."

"Rosary, get the Bishop a Martini!"

Why are all soldiers tired on the lst of April?

Because they have had a thirty-one-day march.

Two businessmen, Mark and Miles, went to a gym for a workout. As they undressed beforehand, Mark was stunned to find Miles wearing a corset beneath his shirt.

"Since when have you been wearing a corset?" asked Miles.

"Since my wife found it in the glove compartment!"

A man went to confession and told the priest, "Father, I am eighty-one, married with six children and thirteen grandchildren, and last night I had an affair and made love to two eighteen-year-olds."

"I see," said the priest. "When was the last time you were in confession?"

"Never, Father," said the old man. "I am Jewish."

"Why are you telling me?"

"I'm telling everybody!"

A lady goes into a soft-furnishing shop: “I am returning this rug I bought from you last week – you promised me it was in mint condition.”

“So it is, madam – with a little hole in the middle!”

A guy approached a very attractive girl in the supermarket: “I have lost my wife. Can I talk to you?”

“Why?” she asked.

“Because every time I talk to a pretty girl my wife appears out of nowhere!”

IF WE DON’T SUCCEED WE RUN THE RISK OF FAILURE.

A guy goes to a psychologist.

"I don't feel well at all," he says.

The psychologist says, "What do you feel like?"

The guy says, "One day I feel like a wigwam and the next I feel like a tepee!"

"No problem," says the psychologist: "you are too tense!"

A guy bought a pair of shoes and said to the salesman, "They are too tight."

"Try them with the tongue out," said the salesman.

"They are thtill too tight," said the guy.

The Mother Superior was discussing the rise in crime rate with one of her nuns.

"Sister," she said, "what would you do if you were walking along the street at night and were accosted by a man?"

"I would lift my habit," replied the nun.

The Mother Superior was shocked to hear this.

"Then what would you do?"

"I would tell him to drop his pants."

The Mother Superior was even more shocked.

"And then what would you do?"

"I would run off because I can run a lot faster with my habit up than he could with his pants down!"

A drunk staggered into a bar and sat down next to a priest. The drunk had lipstick on his collar, booze on his breath and a half-bottle of gin sticking out of his pocket. His clothes were heavily stained.

He started reading a newspaper then turned to the priest and said, "What causes arthritis?"

The priest was clearly uncomfortable and responded testily, "It is caused by loose women, too much alcohol, seeking the company of cheap women and having a general contempt for one's fellow man."

"Well, I'll be damned," muttered the drunk.

The priest said, "Well, I'm sorry if I came on a bit strong just then, but how long have you had arthritis?"

"I don't have it, Father," said the drunk, "but I was just reading here that the Pope does!"

BREVITY IS THE SOUL OF LINGERIE.

SLIDE TO OPEN
CAUTION: DO NOT LEAN OUT OF WINDOW

An objectionable woman in a railway carriage has an equally objectionable Pekingese dog on her lap. There is controversy over seating and a man throws the Pekingese out of the window.

Comment from another person in the carriage: "You have thrown the wrong bitch out of the window."

Did you know that the son of the squaw on the hippopotamus is equal to the sons of the squaws on the other two hides?

Man to waiter: "Can I have a whisky and water?" And, later: "Excuse me – what did you put in first, whisky or water?"

"Whisky, sir."

"Good – no doubt I shall get to it in a minute."

On holiday, husband sending wife a telegram: 'Having a lovely time. Wish you were her.'

The difference one letter makes!

I cannot conceive the difference between a man and a woman.

Athletes have muscles in places where the ordinary person hasn't got places.

A man entering a lift saw a lady in the lift, naked except for her handbag and shoes.

"I like your outfit – my wife has one, but it doesn't fit as well."

In an industrial accident a worker lost the first two fingers of his right hand. He was not adequately compensated, and appealed on the basis that he could not say goodbye properly to his foreman.

TO ERR IS HUMAN, BUT TO REALLY FOUL THINGS UP REQUIRES A COMPUTER.

The pen is mightier than the sword and considerably easier to write with.

Contraceptives should be used on every conceivable occasion.

Those who can, teach; those who can't, review.

Marriage is a wonderful institution, but who wants to live in an institution?

A wealthy man met a beautiful girl and he knew straight away that he wanted to marry her, so he proposed to her.

"We don't know anything about each other," she said.

"No matter – we will learn as we go along."

So they agreed, got married and went on an expensive honeymoon at the finest hotel. On the first morning they went to the hotel pool. He climbed to the top diving board and, with an elaborate somersault, plunged into the water to impress his new bride.

"I used to be an Olympic diving champion – I told you we would learn things about each other as we went along."

His wife jumped into the water and proceeded to swim twenty-five lengths of the pool without breaking sweat.

She climbed out and he said, "That was fantastic – were you an Olympic endurance swimmer?"

"No, no," she said. "I was a hooker in Venice and worked on both sides of the canal."

I slept like a log last night and woke up in the fireplace.

Who was the greatest financier that ever lived?

Noah because he was able to float a company when the whole world was in liquidation.

An Irish truck driver came to a low bridge and the clearance said 10' 8". He got out and measured the truck and realised the vehicle was eleven feet tall so he thought to himself, 'I can't see any cops around – let's go for it!'

Why do women have smaller feet than men?

So they can stand nearer to the sink.

SEX IS AN EMOTION IN MOTION.

A man living on the second storey of an apartment block was leaning out of the window one morning to check whether it was raining when a glass eye suddenly fell into his hand. Looking up, he saw a girl peering down from four storeys up.

"Is this yours?" he called.

"Yes," she replied.

"Hold on – I will bring it up to you."

He took the glass eye up to the girl's apartment and she invited him in. They started chatting – she was very grateful to him and asked him out to dinner. After dinner they went back to her flat. Then he suggested they went back to his place and they went to bed.

When she left the following morning he said, "I have to ask, do you act like this with every man you meet?"

"No," she replied, "only those that catch my eye."

A man parks his car on a road outside of town. A girl gets into the car and things start to get exciting. He begins to undo her dress.

"I probably should have mentioned this before, but I am a prostitute and if you want to have sex with me it will cost you £20."

The guy is not happy, but he pays up and afterwards she gets dressed but he just sits in the driver's seat without starting the engine.

"Are we going anywhere?" she asks.

"I should have mentioned this before, but I am a taxi driver and if you want to get back to town it will cost you £30."

A chap arrived at a hotel one night and found that there was only one room available, which he had to share with a stranger.

He was grateful for anything, but the manager said to him, "I'd better warn you that the occupant in the room snores so loudly that the people next door complained."

The chap came down to breakfast the following day and the manager asked how he slept.

He said, "I had a really good night's sleep."

"Well, how is that? What about the snoring?"

"No problem – he was snoring away and I simply went over to him, kissed him on the cheek and said, 'Goodnight, darling.' He sat bolt upright for the rest of the night watching me like a hawk."

A boy promised his girlfriend, "We are going to have a good time on Saturday. I have three tickets for the big game!"

"Why do we need three?" she asked.

"One for your father, one for your mother and one for your kid sister."

The statistics on sanity are that one out of every four people is suffering from some form of mental illness. Think of your three best friends, and if they are OK then it is you!

THE TROUBLE WITH DOING NOTHING IS YOU DON'T KNOW WHEN YOU HAVE FINISHED!

Mick went into the confessional and said to the priest, "Bless me, Father, for I have sinned. I have been with a loose woman."

The priest said, "Oh dear, was it Mary O'Mally?"

"No, Father."

"Was it Bernadette Casey?"

"No, Father."

"Sheila Burn?"

"No, Father."

A few minutes later Mick emerged from the confession box and met his friend Seamus.

"What did you get?"

"Four Our Fathers, five Hail Marys and three good leads!"

A man bought a parrot, but he got really annoyed because it would not stop swearing. As a punishment he put the bird in the freezer.

An hour later the shivering parrot begged to be let out: "I promise never to swear again. I have learnt my lesson, but just tell me one thing: what on earth did that turkey do?"

A man was drowning his sorrows in the bar with a fellow.

"I had it all," he said: "money, beautiful house, fast car, the love of a beautiful woman, and suddenly it was all gone."

"What happened?" asked his companion.

"My wife found out!"

If one synchronised swimmer drowns do the rest have to drown too?

Why is it called a building when it is already built?

Why is there only one Monopolies Commission?

If a lawyer and a taxman were both drowning and you could save only one, would you go to lunch or read the paper?

A man came home from a long business trip and found his son riding a new bicycle.

"Where did you get that money from?" he asked. "It must have cost £200."

"I earned it hiking," said the boy.

"Come on – tell me the truth. Nobody gets that sort of money hiking – where did you really get the cash?"

"Well, it's like this, Dad: every night you were gone Mr Gillespie from the bank would come over to see Mum and he would give me £20 and tell me to take a hike!"

BEHIND EVERY SUCCESSFUL MAN YOU WILL FIND A WOMAN WHO HAS NOTHING TO WEAR.

If Tony Blair had been captain of the *Titanic* he would have persuaded the passengers that he was just stopping to take on ice.

At General Custer's last stand, surrounded by Indians, he decided to have a tot of whisky.

When he opened the bottle a genie appeared, said thanks for releasing him and added, "I give you one wish, but remember – whatever you wish for the Indians must have two. If you want a rifle they get two."

Custer thought for a moment and said, "I will have a glass eye."

At the Yalta conference Churchill, Roosevelt and Stalin were meeting when a genie again appeared and gave them one wish each.

Stalin: "I'd like to see the American Air Force blasted out of the sky."

Roosevelt: "I'd love to see the Russian Navy blasted out of the water."

Churchill: "I'd love a large brandy and a large cigar, but I'm in no hurry – deal with the other two first."

It's easy to read women like an open book using the Braille system.

Did you hear about the scientist who cloned his own genes? He was beside himself.

A man is on his deathbed; his wife is standing next to him.

He says, "I'm remembering the 1914/18 war, when I was gassed, came home, and you were with me, by my side. Then the 1939/45 war, when I was taken prisoner and you were by my side when I returned home. When we opened a business after the war in the East End and went bankrupt, you were with me, by my side, and now you are standing next to me and I am dying. You're just a bloody jinx!"

THERE IS ONLY ONE THING WRONG WITH YOU: YOU ARE VISIBLE.

HYMNS

A chap went to church and when he returned to the office he had a black eye.

When asked how he got it he said, “In church I was standing behind an attractive young lady. When she got up from praying her skirt was caught. I bent forward to release it and she turned round and blacked my eye.”

The following week, he returned to work with two black eyes.

When asked what happened he replied, “I was standing behind the same young lady and when she got up her husband released her skirt and as I realised she didn’t like it I put it back for her.”

Jack called his office and said, “I cannot come to work today. I have a headache and a stomach ache and my legs hurt.”

The boss said, “Do you know something, I really need you today; when I feel sick I go to my wife and tell her to give me sex, and that makes everything better, then I go to work. You try that.”

Two hours later Jack calls his boss and said, “I did what you said and I feel great. I’ll be back soon. By the way, you have a nice house.”

IF YOU CAN’T STAND THE HEAT STAY OUT OF THE KITCHEN.

STAFF DINNER

(A genuine staff circular from 1897)

In order that the comfort of many is not marred by the lack of certain social graces in the few, the following rules must be adhered to:

1. MEN. Clean shirts and underclothes must be worn, boots polished and laces used. The use of string, however well concealed by blacking, will be frowned upon. Brown boots must not be worn.
2. WOMEN. High-necked garments only. Full sleeves. Use of artificial aids to beauty is to be deplored and heads of department are empowered to order the removal of same.
3. At the dinner table: weekly paid workers. As an aid to their comfort of mind, the directors are generously disposed to allow a minimum of table cutlery – i.e. knife, fork and spoon – thus diminishing the embarrassing indecision of which implements to use at the correct time when courses are served to the table.
4. The impulse to belch is to be studiously contained and any member of the weekly paid staff heard doing so will not be invited again. This also applies equally to women.
5. During the speeches silence must be observed and verbal approbation – i.e. "Hear! Hear!" etc. – is to be confined to departmental heads and salaried employees only. Applause is expected to be enthusiastic. Scraping of chairs is expressly forbidden and the quaffing of large quantities of ale before the dinner is to be shunned. No one will be

allowed to excuse himself during the speeches, which are confidently expected to last for two hours.

6. Staff will stand respectfully when the chairman of the board, followed by the board of directors and their ladies, leaves the table.
7. During the dance, staff are reminded that undue and distasteful proximity of partners will be frowned upon. Staff, particularly the weekly paid workers, are advised to keep well away from their superiors whilst on the floor.
8. The directors are fully aware that the geography of toilets gives rise to some disquiet. It has been decided, therefore, in the interest of all, that the following procedure be adopted:

Departmental heads and their ladies: Will use the top landing offices. The toilet marked 'Bought Ledger Only' will be used by the wives of the heads of departments. The other toilet, marked 'Buying Office Only' will be used by the heads of departments themselves.

Weekly paid workers and their women: Must not use any of the above facilities. Women may use the outside lavatories belonging to the garment factory adjacent to their premises. Permission has been obtained from Messrs Lazenby and Lazarus Limited to do so. Men must use the public lavatory that is across the common. When returning, please see that boots are free of mud.

FAMILIARITY BREEDS CONTEMPT AND CHILDREN.

There was once a zebra who paid a visit to a farm. The first animal he saw was a cow.

He walked up to the cow and said, "I'm a zebra – what are you?"

The cow said, "I'm a cow."

The zebra said, "What do you do?"

The cow said, "Eat a bit of grass and give a few pints of milk."

"Oh," said the zebra and walked away.

He then came upon a chicken.

"Hello. I'm a zebra – what are you?"

"I'm a chicken."

"And what do you do?"

"I eat bits and pieces of corn and give a few eggs."

"Oh," said the zebra and walked away.

The zebra then encountered a bull.

"I'm a zebra – what are you?"

"I'm a bull."

"And what do you do?"

"Well, if you take those striped pyjamas off I'll show you."

An army sergeant was sitting at a desk interviewing recruits.

"Name?"

"McCoy."

"And what are you?"

"I'm a poof."

"Oh, so you're a poof, are you?"

"Yes, I work in a candle factory and go poof."

"Next!"

"McCoy."

"And what do you do?"

"I'm a poof."

"I suppose you work in a candle factory."

"Oh no, I work in a balloon factory and all day long I go poof, blowing up balloons."

"Next!"

"McCoy."

"I suppose you work in a candle or balloon factory?"

"No, I'm the real McCoy."

There was once a chap who had so much bad luck that if he fell in a barrel of breasts he reckoned he would come up sucking his thumb.

Company sales manager conducting a sales talk to members of his staff: "The most important things in business are integrity and wisdom."

A young salesman said, "How do you define integrity and wisdom?"

"Integrity is keeping your promises to the customers even if it means losing money, and wisdom is knowing enough to not make stupid promises in the first place!"

A four-foot-six fortune teller escaped from prison. The announcement on the police radio was "Be on the lookout for a small medium at large."

IS THE LAST GUY TO LET YOU DOWN THE UNDERTAKER?

A guy goes to the Doctor for a medical and takes off his socks.
The Doctor asks, "What's wrong?"
"I have got scarlet feeta."
"No, you mean scarlet fever."
The doctor looks at his knees and asks what is wrong.
"I've got German kneesles."
"No, it's German measles."
Thereupon the Doctor looks at another part of his anatomy.
"You have got small cox."

He is a man of few words, which he uses over and over and over again.

There were two surgeons talking.
"Who are the easiest people you can operate on?"
"Well, if I was operating on a mechanical engineer, an electrical engineer and a politician, the politician would be easiest. When you open up a mechanical engineer or an electrical engineer all the parts are colour-coded. However, it is even easier with a politician because there are only two parts, his mouth and his backside, and they are both interchangeable."

At a dinner a bishop is seated next to a very high-ranking religious temperate character.

A wine waitress appears and says to the Bishop, “Red or white?”

The Bishop says, “Red.”

Then she asks the temperate character, “Red or white?”

“Good God,” he replies, “I would rather commit adultery than let alcohol pass my lips.”

The Bishop says to the waitress, “You didn’t give me that choice.”

The manager of a very large insurance company had to call in a plumber, who did the job in six minutes and charged £75.

The insurance-company manager said, “That’s £7.50 an hour – far more than I earn as a manager of a large insurance company.”

Thereupon the plumber said, “It is far more than I used to earn as manager of an insurance company!”

IT IS GREAT TO BE APPLAUDED IN AND NOT TO BE CLAPPED OUT.

Who said, "We will fight them on the beaches. We will never surrender"?

Answer: Winston Churchill.

Who said, "They have never had it so good"?

Answer: Harold Macmillan.

Who said: "Without defeat there is no profit"?

Answer: An Indian chiropodist.

Men sometimes think of their wives as advisers. On a quiz show on American TV an Englishman was taking part and he was allowed to have a professional adviser. He chose a Frenchman. The Englishman had to kiss a woman three times.

For $1,000, he was asked, "Where would you kiss her first?"

He answered, "On the forehead," which was the right answer.

Tremendous applause.

For $5,000 he was then asked where he would kiss her the second time, and he answered, "On the lips," which was right again.

For $10,000 he was then asked where he would kiss her the third time.

Standing there, slightly nonplussed, he then turned to his professional adviser and asked, "Where?"

The Frenchman replied, "I don't know – I was wrong on the first two!"

After a three-month golfing tour in America a professional golfer was home in bed with his wife, making up for his absence. Their romantic reunion was suddenly interrupted by a knocking at the door.

"Good Lord, that must be your husband!" said the golfer, jumping out of bed and fumbling for his trousers.

"Oh no, it can't be," said the wife; "he's in America playing golf."

The vicar had been badly beaten at golf by a parishioner some thirty years his senior. He returned to the clubhouse disappointed, very depressed.

"Cheer up," said the parishioner. "Remember, you'll win at the finish – you'll probably bury me someday."

"Yeah, but even then," said the vicar, "it would still be your hole."

W. C. Fields was asked if he believed in clubs for women. "Yes," he answered, "if every other form of persuasion fails."

IS CONSTIPATION TO HAVE AND TO HOLD?

GROWING PROBLEM

The film director gazed in despair at his male star's ever growing girth.

"You'll have to go on a diet or your costume won't fit by the time we're halfway through shooting. If that stomach was on the leading lady I'd say she was pregnant."

"I've got news for you, chum," the actor grinned: "it has been and she is."

PROFESSIONAL MATTER

A vicar, a doctor and a lawyer were sitting in a leaky lifeboat after their ship went down and they knew they would sink if they didn't lighten the load. So they drew lots to choose who should dive overboard and swim for it, hoping to reach land before the sharks got him. The lawyer lost and over he went.

Suddenly there were sharks' fins as far as the eye could see, but instead of dividing him up for dinner the sharks lined up on either side of him as a protective escort. The vicar thought it was a miracle; the doctor thought it was just professional courtesy.

CAMERA CASE

In the middle of an assault case, the judge decided that to protect the reputation of the young lady involved he should hear the rest of the evidence in camera.

As the court was cleared the prisoner protested suspiciously: "I don't understand what all this camera business is about."

The judge said frostily, "I understand what it means, learned counsel understand what it means and the jury understands what it means. All you have to do is to go on with your evidence."

"Like I was saying, there we were, all alone in her flat, so I thought I was in with a bit of a chance . . ."

"A bit of a chance?" The judge looked pained. "And what might that mean?"

"Well, Your Honour, I know what it means, learned counsel know what it means, the jury knows what it means and if you'd been there with your perishing camera you'd know what it means!"

A long-distance lorry driver went into a transport café and ordered sausage and chips and a piece of apple pie, and while he was waiting for the food he chatted to the pretty waitress. Just as his order arrived, the door crashed open and in came three great hulking motorcyclists, skulls and crossbones on their helmets and muscles bulging under their leather jackets. They overturned chairs and they shouted rude remarks at the waitress. Then they noticed the lorry driver in the corner. They stood round him in a circle and the leader took a fork, speared the sausage off his plate and ate it. The second biker grabbed a handful of chips and the third tucked into his apple pie. The lorry driver didn't say a word – he just got up and walked quietly out of the café.

"That soon got rid of him," the leader said, leering at the waitress. "Not much of a man, is he?"

"He's not much of a driver either," remarked the waitress. "He's just backed his lorry over three motorcycles."

SPELLBOUND

A lorry driver saw a pretty young woman with long dark hair standing at a bus stop in the pouring rain and he stopped to offer her a lift.

"That's very kind of you," she said, "but I have to warn you that I'm a witch and if you take me with you in your cab anything can happen."

The lorry driver grinned and said he'd take a chance, so she climbed in beside him. Five minutes later she touched him on the knee and he turned into a lay-by.

SEX DISCRIMINATION

An English colonel was dining in a Paris restaurant when he found a fly baked into his pâté. Angrily he summoned the waiter.

Pointing, he said, "*Regardez le mouche.*"

"Eet ees *la mouche*, monsieur, because eet ees feminine," said the waiter, intent on improving his customer's French.

"By Jove, what fantastic eyesight – to tell its sex at that distance!" exclaimed the Colonel.

A young couple had just got married and the guy thought he would show his wife who was boss.

On the first night of the honeymoon he took his trousers off and he said to his wife, "Put those on." She put them on and he said, "Right, that's the first and last time you wear the trousers in our marriage."

"Oh," she said. She then took her pants off, threw them across to him and said, "Now put those on."

The guy said, "I will never be able to get into these."

She replied, "And you never will unless you change your attitude."

THE ELEVENTH COMMANDMENT: THOU SHALT NOT BE FOUND OUT.

An eagle was flying around the sky when he saw a little dove on the ground. He thought to himself, 'This is interesting,' so he flew down and had his way with the dove.

The dove said, "I am a little dove and I have had a little love and I like it."

The eagle then saw a blue tit, so he flew down and had his way with the blue tit.

The blue tit said, "I am a little tit; I had a little bit and I like it."

Half an hour later he saw a duck on the ground and he flew down and had his way with the duck and the duck said, "I am a little drake; he made a mistake, but I like it."

A man driving along in his chauffeur-driven car saw a man on the roadside eating grass.

He stopped the car and said to the man, "Why are you eating grass?"

He said, "I have no money for food."

"Oh," said the man with the car. "Please get in the car and come back with me."

"I have my wife and two children with me and a friend who has a wife and six children."

"No problem – get in the car."

On the way back to the house one of the men said, "Thank you so much indeed for taking us back to your house."

"No, it is me who should thank you – the grass at my house is three foot high."

There was a robbery at the police station – nothing was taken except the lavatories. The police spokesman said they had nothing to go on.

Police arrested two kids yesterday; one was drinking battery acid and the other was eating fireworks. They charged one and let the other off!

NEVER PRACTISE TWO VICES AT ONCE.

I was walking across the fields with my double-barrelled shotgun when I bumped into a guy who said, "Why do you have two barrels on the gun?"

I replied, "If I miss the rabbit with the first one I get it with the second one."

He replied, "Why don't you use the second one first?"

Henry, Paddy and Amos were in Rome, walking along at night. They stumbled over a body, which turned out to be the Pope. They took him back to the Vatican.

A cardinal said, "It's the Pope and he is dead, but we must keep it quiet for forty-eight hours."

They all agreed, and as they were all going home Amos said, "We could make some money on this at the betting office."

Two weeks later they met again.

Amos said, "I am a multimillionaire and won't have to work again."

Henry said, "I've made enough money to keep me comfortable all my life."

Paddy said, "I'm broke."

Amos and Henry both asked, "Why?"

"I bet on a double with the Archbishop of Canterbury."

A golfer was poised over his shot for ages.

"Hurry up," said his partner.

"But my wife is watching from the clubhouse and I want to make this a perfect shot."

"Forget it – you'll never hit her from here!"

A PESSIMIST IS ONE WHO WHEN HE HAS THE CHOICE OF TWO EVILS CHOOSES BOTH.